STEPS TOWARD BALANCING LIFE'S DEMANDS

ABOUT THE AUTHORS

David Durey has been a committed discipler, equipper and mentor for more than 15 years. He believes that leadership development and accelerated spiritual growth are natural by-products of one-to-one discipling, equipping and mentoring relationships.

David has been a pastor in three local churches since 1980. He joined Pastor Dale Galloway in 1990 to serve as a Geographic District Pastor at New Hope Community Church in Portland, Oregon, a church recognized for its use of small groups and Lay Pastors.

Pastor Durey received his Master of Divinity from the International School of Theology, San Bernardino, California. At ISOT he was exposed to some of the finest discipling, equipping and mentoring strategies in the church today.

David has authored *Steps Toward Spiritual Growth*, and co-authored and edited *Steps Toward Ministry*. He has consulted with dozens of churches and church leaders regarding small groups and discipleship. He has also served as a "mentor" to graduate students at Multnomah Biblical Seminary, Portland, Oregon.

Dr. Chuck Goldberg is a Family Physician and business developer in Portland, Oregon, where he also serves as a Lay Pastor Leader at New Hope Community Church. He has been a student of mentoring for more than 10 years, and has mentored others in business and friendship.

Chuck received his Bachelor of Science degree at the University of Michigan, and his Master of Science and Medical Doctorate from the University of Illinois College of Medicine.

Among his mentors, Chuck has been blessed by his father, Bernie, his Physician counselor Truman Anderson, his business associates Ross Hall and Theron Nelsen, and his pastor, David Durey.

Dr. Goldberg has authored many biomedical and wellness articles and contributed to the development and testing of *Steps Toward Spiritual Growth*. He has discipled and mentored dozens of business leaders throughout the Portland area and around the United States.

STEPS TOWARD BALANCING LIFE'S DEMANDS

ONE-TO-ONE MENTORING FOR EFFECTIVE LIVING

DAVID D. DUREY
&
DR. CHUCK GOLDBERG

FOUNDATION OF HOPE
PORTLAND, OREGON

First Printing, January 1995 as *Mentoring for Leadership Development*
Revised edition, March 1997 as *Steps Toward Balancing Life's Demands*

NOTE TO MENTORS: The mentoring workbook you now hold in your hand will allow you to focus your efforts in getting to know your protégé. This tool with its self-evaluation and progress checklist, is flexible and protégé centered.   The ultimate goal is the multiplication of leaders who will in turn mentor others.

FOUNDATION OF HOPE

11731 SE Stevens Road
Portland, Oregon 97266
888-248-3545
(503) 659-5683

Steps Toward Balancing Life's Demands: One-to-one Mentoring for Effective Living
ISBN: 0-9656237-1-8

CONTENTS

ACKNOWLEDGMENTS

We are grateful to God for the following individuals and organizations who have had a tremendous impact and influence on our lives and on the content and creation of this mentoring workbook:

TRUMAN ANDERSON, ROSS HALL AND THERON NELSEN. Key mentors and friends for Chuck.

BOB BIEHL, JERRY "CHIP" MACGREGOR, & GLEN URQUHART, Authors of the booklet, "Mentoring, How to Find a Mentor and How to Become One" available through Masterplanning Group International, Box 952499, Lake Mary, Florida 32795, Telephone (407) 330-2028.

DR. RAY COTTON, Senior Pastor of New Hope Community Church, Portland, Oregon. For his personal encouragement and his shared passion for one-to-one discipleship, mentoring and leadership development.

PASTOR DENNIS DEARDORFF, New Hope Community Church, Portland, Oregon. For his assistance in confirming discipleship and mentoring principles through the men's ministry of New Hope.

KEITH DRURY, RICHARD LAUBY AND CHUCK YONKMAN. Key mentors and friends for David.

GEORGE DUREY AND BERNIE GOLDBERG. Our fathers, who mentored us for living lives of integrity and honor.

DR. DALE E. GALLOWAY, Founding Pastor of New Hope Community Church, Portland, Oregon and Dean of the Beeson Center, Asbury Theological Seminary, Wilmore, Kentucky. One who has dedicated his life to reaching the unchurched thousands through equipping and releasing God's people for service.

PASTOR JUDY KENNEDY, New Hope Community Church, Portland, Oregon. For her heart for mentoring women and her assistance in testing mentoring principles through the women's ministry of New Hope.

PASTOR WENDELL MORTON, Promise Keepers, Boulder, Colorado. A partner in the vision of mentoring for leadership development in order to change our world one person at a time.

FOREWORD

Dr. Chuck Goldberg and pastor David Durey have both been passion-
ate in the pursuit of mentoring and growing strong healthy leaders.

In successful mentoring or leadership development you have to pay
attention to these three things: spiritual formation, how to do ministry, and a balanced healthy life. In this tested and proven tool, all
three areas blend into growing a leader. This unique and special tool
has been forged on the anvil of experience. Thank God for this won-
derful tool to help us do a better job in mentoring and leadership
development.

"Build leaders and they will build ministries."

Dr. Dale Galloway
Dean of the Beeson Center for Church Leadership
Asbury Theological Seminary
Wilmore, Kentucky

ONE-TO-ONE MENTORING

STEPS TOWARD BALANCING LIFE'S DEMANDS

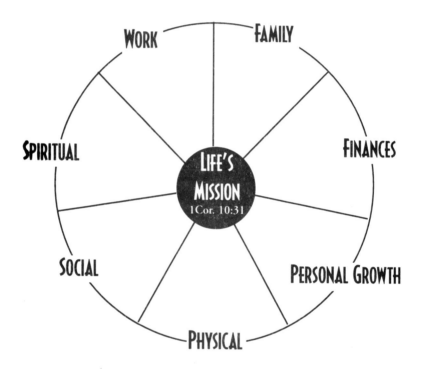

"*Emerging leaders need the support of a mentor and the account-ability that comes from being a mentor to their own protégé — they need someone to follow and someone to lead.*"

INTRODUCTION

WHAT IS MENTORING?

Mentoring has become a popular term during recent years. However, it is difficult, if not impossible to find one standard definition. In his book, Mentoring, Bob Biehl suggests that, "Mentoring is a lifelong relationship, in which a mentor helps a protégé reach her or his God-given potential."[1] Paul Stanley and J. Robert Clinton state that, "Mentoring is a relational experience in which one person empowers another by sharing God-given resources."[2]

The booklet, Mentoring: How to Find a Mentor and How to Become One, offers the simple analogy of a mentor as one who is like a loving older brother or sister who seeks the best for the younger brother or sister over the course of time.[3] The tools that a mentor brings to the relationship are experience, wisdom, resources and a network of other capable people. The mentor allows these tools to be used to help the younger brother or sister reach their goals and grow to their full potential. The one being mentored is called the protégé. This younger brother or sister is looking to the mentor as a model, helper and encourager. The mentor does not use the protégé to achieve the mentor's own personal goals. Nor, is the mentor trying to make the protégé just like him or her. Instead, the mentor asks two questions:

1. Where is it that you want to go in life?
2. How can I help you get there?

EXAMPLES FROM THE BIBLE

Mentoring is a powerful relational principle that has shaped lives throughout human history. The Bible offers many mentoring examples. In Genesis 12-14 and 18-19 Abraham, the patriarch of the Jews, demonstrates a mentoring relationship with his nephew Lot. The books of Exodus, Numbers and Deuteronomy record the mentoring relationship of Moses, the nation's leader, and Joshua, his successor. Other prominent Old Testament mentoring relationships include Elijah and Elisha (1 Kings 19:19-21, 2 Kings 2:1-5) and Naomi and Ruth (Ruth 1-3).

New Testament examples of mentoring include two important women, Elizabeth, the mother of John the Baptist, and her younger cousin, Mary, the mother of our Lord Jesus Christ. Jesus had many disciples but He also selected Peter, James and John to be in His inner circle. For instance, only these three witnessed Jesus on the mount of His transfiguration (Matthew 17:1-13). Other prominent mentoring relationships include Barnabas and Paul (Acts 9:26-30, 11:25-26, 13:1-15:41) and Paul and Timothy (Acts 16:1-3, 1 & 2 Timothy).

TYPES OF MENTORS

In their book, *Connecting*, Paul Stanley and J. Robert Clinton offer an expanded view of mentoring which identifies seven types of mentoring functions ranging from intensive relationships which are the most deliberate to passive relationships which are the least deliberate.[4] Read through the information below and see if you can identify the mentoring relationships that you have had in your life.

MENTORING TYPES	CENTRAL THRUST OF EMPOWERMENT
1. **Intensive**	
Discipler	Enablement in basics of following Christ.
Spiritual Guide	Accountability, direction, and insight for personal growth, spirituality and maturity.
Coach	Motivation, skills, and application needed to meet a task or challenge.
2. **Occasional**	
Counselor	Timely advice and correct perspectives on viewing self, others, and ministry.
Teacher	Gives knowledge, understanding and insights regarding a particular subject.
Sponsor	Career guidance, protection and support within an organization.
3. **Passive (Models)**	
Contemporary	A person whose life and ministry currently serve as an example and inspiration.
Historical	A past life that teaches dynamic principles and values for life, ministry, and/or profession.

HOW TO USE THIS MENTORING WORKBOOK

This mentor-protégé workbook is designed to help you establish a more deliberate and intensive mentoring relationship. It will allow you to get to know your protégé and evaluate how you can best help him or her succeed in every area of life.

STEP 1. SELECT A PROTÉGÉ

Select someone whom you admire, love, and believe in. In this context, men should only mentor men and women should only mentor women. The protégé should be teachable, self-motivated, and have a desire to grow. Also, ask yourself if you enjoy spending time with this person. Are you threatened or uncomfortable with them in any way? Start with one protégé and do not exceed more than three at one time.

STEP 2. EXPLAIN MENTORING TO THE PROTÉGÉ

Invite the protégé to begin a mentoring relationship by making a six month to one year mentor-protégé commitment. Review the Progress Checklist and give an overview of the book. Also, explain that the protégé should consider becoming a mentor to others sometime in the future.

STEP 3. DISCUSS THE SELF-EVALUATION

Have your protégé complete the Self-Evaluation worksheets and discuss them at your first mentoring appointment:

___ People
___ Pinciples Learned
___ Personal Time-Line
___ Possessions and Purpose
___ Seven Areas of Life Management

STEP 4. DISCUSS YOUR PROTÉGÉ'S FOCUS

Help your protégé identify possessions such as their unique personality type, present opportunities, and personal resources. Also assist your protégé in writing a personal mission statement.

___ Possessions: What Has God Entrusted To You?
___ Purpose: What is God's Call on Your Life?

STEP 5. DISCUSS THE SEVEN AREAS OF LIFE MANAGEMENT

Read and discuss the key biblical principles, then take inventory of
the protégé's roles, objectives, goals and disciplines in each of the
Seven Areas of Life Management.[5] Meet regularly until you have
studied all the key biblical principles and completed the inventory
worksheets for the following Seven Areas of Life Mangement:

- __ Family (marriage and children)
- __ Finances (sharing, spending, saving)
- __ Personal Growth (mental & emotional)
- __ Physical (health and fitness)
- __ Social (friendship and citizenship)
- __ Spiritual (seeking and serving God)
- __ Work (personal contribution)

STEP 6. SUPPORT YOUR PROTÉGÉ'S SUCCESS

After completing all the worksheets for Possessions, Purpose, Seven
Areas of Life Management and Balancing Life's Demands, continue to
meet regularly (weekly, bimonthly, monthly) for at least six months to
one year using the Mentoring Checklist as a guide for your discus-
sions.

YOUR MENTORING COMMITMENT

We are making a six month to one year mentor-protégé commitment
and a lifetime commitment to mentor others.

Mentor: _____ Date: _____

Protégé: _____ Date: _____

PROGRESS CHECKLIST

SELF-EVALUATION Date covered: __/__/__
- ☐ Personal Time-Line
- ☐ Possessions and Purpose
- ☐ Seven Areas of Life Management

POSSESSIONS Date covered: __/__/__
- ☐ Personality
- ☐ Present Opportunities
- ☐ Personal Resources

PURPOSE Date covered: __/__/__
- ☐ Personal Destiny
- ☐ Personal Mission Statement

FAMILY Date covered: __/__/__
- ☐ Discussed Key Principles
- ☐ Identified Roles
- ☐ Defined Objective
- ☐ Set Specific Goals

FINANCES Date covered: __/__/__
- ☐ Discussed Key Principles
- ☐ Identified Roles
- ☐ Defined Objective
- ☐ Set Specific Goals

PERSONAL GROWTH Date covered: __/__/__
- ☐ Discussed Key Principles
- ☐ Identified Roles
- ☐ Defined Objective
- ☐ Set Specific Goals

PHYSICAL Date covered: ___/___/___
- ☐ Discussed Key Principles
- ☐ Identified Roles
- ☐ Defined Objective
- ☐ Set Specific Goals

SOCIAL Date covered: ___/___/___
- ☐ Discussed Key Principles
- ☐ Identified Roles
- ☐ Defined Objective
- ☐ Set Specific Goals

SPIRITUAL Date covered: ___/___/___
- ☐ Discussed Key Principles
- ☐ Identified Roles
- ☐ Defined Objective
- ☐ Set Specific Goals

WORK Date covered: ___/___/___
- ☐ Discussed Key Principles
- ☐ Identified Roles
- ☐ Defined Objectives
- ☐ Set Specific Goals

BALANCING LIFE'S DEMANDS Date covered: ___/___/___
- ☐ Discussed Key Principles
- ☐ Set Standard Weekly Schedule

MENTORING CHECKLIST Date covered: ___/___/___
- ☐ Sample Session

SELF-EVALUATION

(LOOKING BACK)

PEOPLE

1. Who are the key people in your life that have made a positive impact on you?

2. What other individuals have been influential in your life whether or not you knew them personally?

3. Describe your closest friends at this time.

PRINCIPLES LEARNED

1. What are three key principles you have learned in life?

2. What personal beliefs do you have that you are convinced to be universally true?

3. What beliefs would you be willing to die for?

PERSONAL TIME-LINE

1. What are the key elements that mark your life up to this time? (successes, hardships, education, spiritual experience, etc.)

2. How would you label or describe the different stages or segments of your life to this point? Create a time-line to illustrate your answer.

    Childhood
    | --->

    Youth
    | --->

    Young Adult
    | --->

    Adult
    | --->

POSSESSIONS   Low   High

1. I have taken a serious look at what God has   1 2 3 4 5
   entrusted to me and I am seeking to use my
   possessions to His glory.

2. I am aware of my basic personality.   1 2 3 4 5

3. I have taken a recent accounting of my present   1 2 3 4 5
   opportunities for service.

4. I am aware of my personal resources: talents,   1 2 3 4 5
   skills and spiritual gifts.

PURPOSE

1. I have thought about the purpose that God has   1 2 3 4 5
   for my life.

2. I have identified my personal passions and   1 2 3 4 5
   priorities.

3. I am aware of God's will for all Christians as   1 2 3 4 5
   revealed in the Bible.

4. I have written a personal statement of purpose.   1 2 3 4 5

SEVEN AREAS OF LIFE MANAGEMENT

1. All of the pieces of your life can be categorized under one of
   seven basic areas and everything you do in one area effects
   the others.[1] Rate yourself in each of the Seven Areas of Life
   Management:

	Low			High	
Family (marriage and family)	1	2	3	4	5
Finances (sharing, spending, saving)	1	2	3	4	5
Personal Growth (mental and emotional)	1	2	3	4	5
Physical (health and fitness)	1	2	3	4	5
Social (friendship and citizenship)	1	2	3	4	5
Spiritual (seeking and serving God)	1	2	3	4	5
Work (personal contribution)	1	2	3	4	5

2. To which of the seven areas have you been giving too much time, energy or money?

3. Which areas have you neglected?

4. In which area do you feel the most pressure? Why?

5. What unwanted results may occur if you continue living your life as you are currently?

POSSESSIONS

WHAT HAS GOD ENTRUSTED TO YOU?

POSSESSION 1: PERSONALITY

Every person has a unique God-given personality. Most personality inventories identify four basic categories.[1] Every person is a unique blend of these four and there is no bad, good, better or best personality type. Every personality is good and each is needed. Each personality is a unique combination of strengths and weaknesses and every person is most effective when they are able to match their unique strengths with their life situations. Take the personality inventory below to help you identify your primary and secondary personality types.

A PERSONALITY INVENTORY

Circle the words in each section that you believe describe a quality that is true about you. Then count the total number circled in each category and multiply that number by two. Record your score on the following page.

1. **The "T" personality**

Diplomatic	Tactful	Logical
Hard working	Thorough	Orderly
High self-expectations	Conscientious	Disciplined
Precise	Analytical	Hesitant
Rejects lack of quality	Pessimistic	Reserved
Factual	Detailed	Calculating
Inquisitive	High standards	Collect data
Recognize authority	Discerning	Scheduled

Total "T" score. Double the number circled_____

2. **The "A" personality**

Problem solver	Takes charge	Impatient
Enjoys challenges	Goal driven	Demanding
Competitive	Risk taker	Assertive
Value results	Reject inaction	Confident
Direct	Task oriented	Impulsive
Dominant	Bored easily	Variety
Freedom to act	Decisive	Persistent
Poor listener	Achiever	Independent

Total "A" score. Double the number circled_____

3. **The "P" personality**

Optimistic	Expressive	Fun-loving
Entertaining	Value recognition	Avoid isolation
Persuasive	Generous	Enthusiastic
Group oriented	Dreamers	Enjoy change
Motivator	Avoids details	Over-selling
Energetic	Promoters	Like variety
People helpers	Over committed	Articulate
Lack follow-through	Intuitive	Creative

Total "P" score. Double the number circled_____

4. **The "S" personality**

Cooperative	Calm	Loyal
Lack confidence	Value relationships	Sympathetic
Supportive	Agreeable	Consistent
Good listener	Self-controlled	Resist change
Procrastinator	Indecisive	Avoid conflict
Tolerant	Enjoy routine	Patient
Team player	Polite	Warm/agreeable
Difficult to say "no"	Family oriented	Kind

Total "S" score. Double the number circled_____

IDENTIFYING YOUR PERSONALITY TYPE

1. Transfer your scores from the personality inventory to the scoring chart below. Circle the number that is closest to your total score for each of the four personality categories.

	Not My Type!								Perfect Match!
"T" - Thinker	5....10....15....20....25....30....35....40....45....50
"A" - Achiever	5....10....15....20....25....30....35....40....45....50
"P" - Promoter	5....10....15....20....25....30....35....40....45....50
"S" - Supporter	5....10....15....20....25....30....35....40....45....50

2. Write the names of your primary and secondary personality types below.

_____   _____
Primary personality (highest score) - Secondary personality

THE FOUR PERSONALITY TYPES

Read the descriptions of your primary and secondary personality listed below. Circle or underline the items listed under your primary and secondary personality that you feel are true of you.[2]

1. **The THINKER.** "Let's do it right."
   They enjoy proven methods and tasks that are completed with attention to high quality. They value high quality and getting things done correctly. They are diplomatic, tactful, logical, hard working and thorough. They are able to focus on details. They can struggle with decision making and perfectionism. They tend to have high expectations of both themselves and others.

2. **The ACHIEVER.** "Let's get it done."
   They enjoy difficult challenges. They value results but reject inaction. They are confident, direct, persistent, productive and good problem solvers. They are more oriented toward tasks than relationships and they can struggle with being too impulsive, too dominant or getting bored too easily. They tend to be detached and independent and struggle with being a good listener.

3. **The PROMOTER.** "Let's make it fun and exciting."
    They enjoy involvement in influencing others toward an exciting goal or a worthwhile cause. They are relational, optimistic, expressive, fun-loving and often entertaining in nature. They value recognition and approval and tend to avoid isolation. They can struggle with organization and a disciplined lifestyle. They tend to focus on the future and often want to rush to the next exciting challenge before the present task is complete.

4. **The SUPPORTER.** "You can depend on me."
    They enjoy participation and close relationships with a select group of friends. They avoid conflict. They struggle with saying "no" when asked to take on a responsibility. They are oriented toward people and maintaining a good environment. They are warm, friendly and good listeners. They are cooperative, calm, patient and loyal. They can struggle with accepting changes and a lack of confidence. They value good relationships and appreciation and often have higher expectations of themselves than they do of others.

POSSESSION 2: PRESENT OPPORTUNITIES

God has allowed you to be in your present circumstances. You may have sought His guidance and direction as you arrived at this point or you may have tried to direct your life according to your own will and design. Either way, you have the opportunity to allow God to be your help and guide from this time forward.

OPPORTUNITIES TO OBEY

1. Are there any areas or aspects of your life that you realize are not pleasing to God? If so, what are they?

2. Are you willing to accept the challenge of committing these areas to God and changing them with His help and power?

OPPORTUNITIES TO HELP

1. In what areas of personal interest or concern do you currently have the opportunity to contribute time, energy, expertise or resources?

2. What are you presently doing in these areas?

3. What challenges or problems have you identified that you feel you might be able to help solve?

POSSESSION 3: PERSONAL RESOURCES

TALENTS AND SKILLS

1. What have other people suggested that you do well?

2.   What do you feel are some of your personal talents or skills?

SPIRITUAL GIFTS

What spiritual gifts do you know that you possess? From the following list taken from the discipleship book, *Steps Toward Spiritual Growth*, circle those gifts that you feel you have used effectively in the past.[3]

Helps	Leadership	Hospitality
Service	Administration	Discernment
Faith	Music	Languages (Tongues)
Miracles	Craftsmanship	Healing
Giving	Mercy	Wisdom
Knowledge	Exhortation	Teaching
Pastor/Shepherd	Apostleship	Missionary
Prophecy	Evangelism	Intercession

OTHER RESOURCES

What additional resources are at your disposal? (consider such things as finances, friendships, networks, family, influence, special knowledge, athletic ability, high energy, analytical skills, etc.)

MANAGE WHAT GOD HAS GIVEN

Whatever God has entrusted to you, use it for His glory. Review this lesson and take inventory of all that God has entrusted to you. Say a prayer of thanks to God and determine to use everything you have to His glory and honor.

PURPOSE

WHAT IS GOD'S CALL ON YOUR LIFE?

PERSONAL DESTINY

PERSONAL PASSION

1. What are the three things that you value most in life?

2. Do you have one or more consuming dreams or visions? If so, what are they?

3. If you could be assured of success in any venture, what major accomplishments would you achieve in your lifetime?

4. Where do you sense God is leading your life?

5. How do you see yourself in 10, 20 or 30 years?

    10 years

    20 years

    30 years

PERSONAL PRIORITIES

1. What virtues or character qualities do you aspire to develop
    during your lifetime? (Circle no more than 10)

Caring	Compassionate	Confident
Considerate	Consistent	Contented
Cooperative	Courageous	Creative
Dedicated	Dependable	Diligent
Enthusiastic	Fair	Flexible
Forgiving	Friendly	Generous
Gentle	Giving	Helpful
Honest	Humble	Joyful
Kind	Loving	Loyal
Merciful	Obedient	Patient
Peaceful	Reliable	Respectful
Responsible	Self-controlled	Self-disciplined
Sensitive	Sincere	Supportive
Teachable	Thankful	Tolerant
Trusting	Trustworthy	Unselfish

2. List 5-10 things that you hope to obtain during your life?
    1.
    2.
    3.
    4.
    5.
    6.

3. Who are the 5-10 individuals or groups that you hope to help during the course of your life?
    1.
    2.
    3.
    4.
    5.
    6.

4. What are the 5-10 major accomplishments that you hope to have achieved during your life?
    1.
    2.
    3.
    4.
    5.
    6.

PERSONAL PERSPECTIVE

1. If you were asked to write your autobiography at the close of your life, what title would you use?

2.   How would you word the major sections or key chapters of your autobiography? (write at least 3-5 chapter titles)

PERSONAL MISSION STATEMENT

BIBLICAL PURPOSE

For a Christian, the place to begin in creating a personal mission statement is a study of the Bible. God has revealed many principles regarding our reason for existence as individuals. No believer should feel that they are living without meaning and purpose for God gives value and worth by the purposes He has declared for those who follow Him.

1.   Study the following Bible references in their context and summarize how they help define God's purposes for those who follow Him.

Matthew 28:19-20

Psalm 37:1-9

Matthew 25:14-30

Mark 10:35-45

Psalm 119:1-16

Matthew 22:34-40

Mark 16:15-16

Philippians 3:8-14

2. List other Bible references and key insights that God has used to guide your life to this point.

3. Read 1 Corinthians 10:31. How could this verse serve as a biblical purpose statement and a personal mission statement for you as a follower of Christ?

YOUR PERSONAL MISSION STATEMENT

A personal mission statement is a reflection of biblical purpose, personal priorities and vision. Biblical purposes will remain unchanged. Your personal priorities can change, but usually remain about the same throughout life (see Priorities and Perspective, pages 26-28). However, your vision, (see Personal Passion, pages 25-26) will likely change as you face new challenges and opportunities in life and as God works within you to accomplish His will through you.

1. There can be great variety in how you write your personal mission statement. This statement can be rewritten and updated as often as you choose. Review your responses in this chapter, then write a personal mission statement below (see examples in Appendix A):

2. Now, summarize your purpose statement in just three words:

FAMILY

(MARRIAGE AND FAMILY)

KEY VERSE: JOSHUA 24:15
"But as for me and my household, we will serve the LORD."

KEY CONCEPT
The family is the institution created by God as the foundation for the preservation of the human race. God intended that children have the guidance of both father and mother. The man should seek to humbly submit to the will and direction of God as he leads and cares for his family. Under this loving leadership, each family member should also maintain an attitude of service to one another, as an act of obedience and love for God (Ephesians 5:21).

LIFE ILLUSTRATION
Tom and Nancy were the perfect image of what a husband and wife should be. Tom worked as an electronics engineer and Nancy, working out of their home, was the premiere computer consultant in the area. They loved each other and their two beautiful children.

Everything was going well until Tom's company was bought out and he was laid off during the corporate downsizing. Then Nancy lost the contract with her largest computer consulting client. At first, it looked like their savings would carry them through, but when Tom couldn't find a new job in the area, they were forced to cut back.

Now Christmas was coming, and each had looked forward to giving the other a special gift that year. Tom enjoyed driving his sports car on dates with Nancy or when taking one of the children on an outing. Nancy had planned for months to buy Tom a new audio system for the car. On the other hand, Tom knew that Nancy had longed to upgrade her computer memory and software.

In spite of the financial difficulties that year, the kids each received what they had checked off on their Christmas lists. However, the scene was the most tender when it was time to open Mom and Dad's gifts for each other. Nancy had tears in her eyes when she opened the package that contained all the upgrades that she had been longing for. Tom burst out in laughter when he opened his gift and saw that ultimate audio system for his automobile.

Tom and Nancy embraced as they each explained how they had found the money to buy their special gifts for each other. Nancy told how she had sold her computer to buy the audio system and Tom explained how he had sold the sports car and used part of the money to buy the computer upgrades. The children joined them that day for a huge "group hug." They realized that the greatest gift received that Christmas was the love and commitment they had for each other.

KEY BIBLICAL PRINCIPLES: FAMILY

THE MARRIAGE RELATIONSHIP

1. **A believer must not marry an unbeliever.** *A woman is bound to her husband as long as he lives. But if her husband dies, she is free to marry anyone she wishes, but he must belong to the Lord.* 1 Corinthians 7:39

2. **God intends marriage to be a permanent union between a man and woman.** *"Haven't you read," he replied, "that at the beginning the Creator 'made them male and female,' and said, 'For this reason a man will leave his father and mother and be united to his wife, and the two will become one flesh'? So they are no longer two, but one. Therefore what God has joined together, let man not separate."* Matthew 19:4-6

3. **A believer should never go into a marriage with the idea that divorce is a valid option if things are not going well.** *Jesus replied, "Moses permitted you to divorce your wives because your hearts were hard. But it was not this way from the*

beginning. I tell you that anyone who divorces his wife, except for marital unfaithfulness, and marries another woman commits adultery." Matthew 19:8-9 (Also see 1 Corinthians 7:12-13)

4. **Sex is a beautiful expression of lifelong commitment that should only be experienced and enjoyed by a man and woman who have entered into the bonds of marriage.**
Marriage should be honored by all, and the marriage bed kept pure, for God will judge the adulterer and all the sexually immoral. Hebrews 13:4 (Also see 1 Corinthians 7:2-5; Proverbs 5:18-19)

5. **The Husband must demonstrate love for his wife by seeking to discover and meet her needs before satisfying his own.**
Husbands, love your wives, just as Christ loved the church and gave himself up for her....In this same way, husbands ought to love their wives as their own bodies. Ephesians 5:25, 28, 33

6. **The wife should encourage her husband to fulfill his leadership responsibilities in the home by showing respect and a willingness to submit to godly leadership.**
Wives, submit to your husbands as to the Lord. For the husband is the head of the wife as Christ is head of the church, his body, of which he is the Savior. Now as the church submits to Christ, so also wives should submit to their husbands in everything. Ephesians 5:22-24 (Also see Colossians 3:18-19)

7. **Husbands and wives must honor one another, living together in love and mutual respect.**
Wives, in the same way be submissive to your husbands so that, if any of them do not believe the word, they may be won over without talk by the behavior of their wives....Husbands, in the same way be considerate as you live with your wives, and treat them with respect as the weaker partner and as heirs with you of the gracious gift of life, so that nothing will hinder your prayers. 1 Peter 3:1, 7

FAMILY RELATIONSHIPS

1. **Children are to honor and obey their parents.** *Children, obey your parents in the Lord, for this is right. "Honor your father and mother" — which is the first commandment with a promise — "that it may go well with you and that you may enjoy long life on the earth."* Ephesians 6:1-3; (Also see Colossians 4:20; Exodus 20:12)

2. **Fathers (Parents) must not exasperate their children and provoke them to anger by using parental authority to make unreasonable demands, petty rules, or show favoritism.** *Fathers, do not exasperate your children; instead, bring them up in the training and instruction of the Lord.* Ephesians 6:4

3. **Children continue in the direction that parents teach and model.** *Train a child in the way he should go, and when he is old he will not turn from it.* Proverbs 22:6

4. **Your children need loving guidance and correction, otherwise, their lives will be destroyed.**
Discipline your son, for in that there is hope; do not be a willing party to his death. Proverbs 19:18.
He who spares the rod hates his son but he who loves him is careful to discipline him. Proverbs 13:24

5. **Parents are to provide spiritual guidance and instruction to their children.** *These commandments that I give you today are to be upon your hearts. Impress them on your children. Talk about them when you sit at home and when you walk along the road, when you lie down and when you get up.* Deuteronomy 6:6-7

TAKING INVENTORY: FAMILY
LIFE LESSONS

1. Who has provided a positive role model for you in the area of Family?

2.   What principles and insights have surfaced from your discussion
     of marriage and family?

ROLES THAT RELATE TO MARRIAGE AND FAMILY

Roles are functions that you perform, areas in which you have responsibilities or in which you play an important and identifiable part.
Examples include being a son, daughter, wife, husband, brother or sister.

1.

2.

3.

DEFINING YOUR LONG-RANGE OBJECTIVE

This statement should be general, non-measurable and non-dated.
Summarize your objective for this area of life by completing this statement: "Over the next 5-10 years I want to . . . ."

SPECIFIC GOALS FOR THIS YEAR

Goals are specific, measurable and time-dated. What two or three
goals do you want to accomplish this year in the area of family?

1.

2.

3.

DISCIPLINES

What positive routines and helpful habits do you need to continue on a regular basis, daily, weekly, or monthly, that will help you remain focused, orderly and efficient?

1.

2.

3.

4.

VICTORIES

What progress or victories have you experienced so far in your efforts to succeed in your family relationships?

CHALLENGES

What challenges are you having in reaching your marriage or family goals?

FINANCES

(SHARING, SPENDING, SAVING)

KEY VERSE: PHILIPPIANS 4:12

"I know what it is to be in need, and I know what it is to have plenty. I have learned the secret of being content in any and every situation, whether well fed or hungry, whether living in plenty or in want."

KEY CONCEPT

God is creator, provider and owner of all things. As humans we must realize that our responsibility to God is that of being stewards or managers of His resources.

LIFE ILLUSTRATION

A teacher and his wife had felt humiliated for years by many unpaid debts. In addition, they were increasingly worried that local merchants might come after them "en mase." Wanting to clear their balances and their consciences, they paid every penny they could squeeze from their income. There seemed to be barely enough to break even. In fact, they felt forced to buy where they could get credit regardless of higher costs.

As you may imagine, this developed into a vicious circle that grew worse instead of better. They began to feel as if there was no hope for them, until a friend made a simple suggestion: list your debts, go to everyone you owe, and explain your situation.

The merchants could see the truth of this couple's "impossible" situation from the figures. The teacher and his wife explained that they would set aside 20 percent of their income each month, divide it among their creditors, and thereby pay everyone in full. In addition, they would live on a cash basis and avoid any further credit purchases.

All agreed, but the grocer put it best when he said, "If you pay for all you buy and then pay some on what you owe, that is better than you've done before!" The couple worked together to live upon 70 percent, determining to tithe and save the other 10 percent.

By cutting costs and looking forward to a debt free future, the adventure continued with the halting of new debt and the clearing of old debt. Soon there was an accumulation of a surplus and a gratifying sense of security for their family's future.

KEY BIBLICAL PRINCIPLES: FINANCES

ACKNOWLEDGE YOUR SOURCE

1. **God is the Creator, Provider, and Owner of all you possess.**
   "The earth is the Lord's and everything in it, the world, and all who live in it." Psalm 24:1

2. **God promises and wants to supply your needs.**
   "And my God will meet all your needs according to his glorious riches in Christ Jesus." Philippians 4:19 (also Psalm 37:25)

3. **You cannot serve both God and money.**
   "No servant can serve two masters. Either he will hate the one and love the other, or he will be devoted to the one and despise the other. You cannot serve both God and Money." Luke 16:13

   "...who alone is immortal and who lives in unapproachable light, whom no one has seen or can see. To Him be honor and might forever. Command those who are rich in this present world not to be arrogant nor to put their hope in wealth, which is so uncertain, but to put their hope in God, who richly provides us with everything for our enjoyment. Command them to do good, to be rich in good deeds, and to be generous and willing to share." 1 Timothy 6:16-18

4. The tithe (10 percent) is given in recognition that God owns it all and has provided all that we have.
    "Bring the whole tithe into the storehouse, that there may be food in my house. Test me in this," says the Lord. "and see if I will not throw open the floodgates of heaven and pour out so much blessing that you will not have room enough for it." Malachi 3:10

    "Honor the Lord with your wealth, with the firstfruits of all your crops; then your barns will be filled to overflowing, and your vats will brim over with new wine." Proverbs 3:9-10

MANAGE YOUR RESOURCES

1. God requires that you obey the civil authority that He has established and that you pay the taxes that are due.
    Everyone must submit himself to the governing authorities for there is no authority except that which God has established. . . . This is also why you pay taxes, for the authorities are God's servants, who give their full time to governing. Give everyone what you owe him: If you owe taxes, pay taxes; if revenue, then revenue; if respect then respect; if honor, then honor. Romans 13:1-7.

2. It is wise to remain free from personal debt.
    The rich rule over the poor, and the borrower is servant to the lender. Proverbs 22:7

3. God expects you to work in order to provide for family needs.
    If anyone does not provide for his relatives, and especially for his immediate family, he is denied the faith and is worse than an unbeliever. 1 Timothy 5:8

4. You should sustain a spirit of contentment and avoid the love of money.
    Keep your lives free from the love of money and be content with what you have because God has said, "Never will I leave you; never will I forsake you." Hebrews 13:5 (also 1 Timothy 6:6-10)

GIVE FREELY

1. **You cannot out-give God.**
    Remember this: Whoever sows sparingly will also reap sparingly, and whoever sows generously will also reap generously. Each man should give what he has decided in his heart to give, not reluctantly or under compulsion, for God loves a cheerful giver. 2 Corinthians 9:6-7

    Give, and it will be given to you. A good measure, pressed down, shaken together and running over, will be poured into your lap. For with the measure you use, it will be measured to you. Luke 6:38

2. **You are to financially support those who are serving in full-time ministry as their primary occupation.**
    In the same way the Lord has commanded that those who preach the gospel should receive their living from the gospel. 1 Corinthians 9:14

3. **Giving to the needs of others should be a major goal for a Christian.**
    If anyone has material possessions and sees his brother in need but has no pity on him, how can the love of God be in him? Dear children, let us not love with words or tongue but with actions and in truth. 1 John 3:17-18 (also Proverbs 3:27-28; Galatians 6:10)

TAKING INVENTORY: FINANCES

LIFE LESSONS

1. Who has provided a positive role model for you in managing finances?

2. What principles and insights have surfaced from your discussion of finances?

ROLES THAT RELATE TO FINANCES

Roles are functions that you perform, areas in which you have responsibilities or in which you play an important and identifiable part. Examples might include primary provider of income, primary money manager, care for feeding or clothing the family.

1.

2.

3.

DEFINING YOUR LONG-RANGE OBJECTIVE

This statement should be general, non-measurable and non-dated. Summarize your objective for this area of life by completing this statement: "Over the next 5-10 years I want to . . . ."

SPECIFIC GOALS FOR THIS YEAR

Goals are specific, measurable and time-dated. What two or three goals do you want to accomplish this year in the area of finances?

1.

2.

3.

DISCIPLINES

What positive routines and helpful habits do you need to continue on a regular basis, daily, weekly, or monthly, that will help you remain focused, orderly and efficient?

1.

2.

3.

4.

VICTORIES

What progress or victories have you experienced so far in your efforts to succeed in your finances.

CHALLENGES

What challenges are you having in reaching your financial goals?

PERSONAL GROWTH

(MENTAL AND EMOTIONAL)

KEY VERSE: PHILIPPIANS 4:8

"Finally, brothers, whatever is true, whatever is noble, whatever is right, whatever is pure, whatever is lovely, whatever is admirable — if anything is excellent or praiseworthy — think about such things."

KEY CONCEPT

God has given us a tremendous capacity to think and feel. However, if we fail to follow God's design, our lives can be filled with great pain and anxiety. God wants us to become all that He created us to be. However, He doesn't expect us to do this alone. He wants to be a partner in sustaining our emotional freedom and developing our unique gifts.

LIFE ILLUSTRATION

Phil was a good boy. He enjoyed sports and school, and did well at both. He also enjoyed being with the family. Phil was a real "go-getter" who put everything he had into the projects and tasks that he had to do. He also felt that his superior efforts and accomplishments merited special rewards for what he considered to be a job well done. He especially enjoyed receiving gifts or money when he had completed a task.

On one particular occasion, Mom and Dad were getting their home ready for a special visit by the grandparents. They had asked Phil to pitch in and help by cleaning the attic. Phil gave it all he had and really did a great job in cleaning the attic. He organized the boxes and made things look better than they ever had before.

When he came downstairs he asked his father, "Well, what do I get for that?" Dad looked at him and said, "Don't you know that you've already received a reward?" Phil didn't quite understand what his father was saying and replied, "No, I don't! I thought you'd give me a couple of tickets to the basketball game, or at least pay me $10 or $20 for doing that job." Dad looked a little bit deflated as he said to him, "Phil, your brothers, your mother and I all worked on this together. The reward that we already received is personal satisfaction." Phil look puzzled and frustrated as he walked back to his room.

Many months later, after the "attic" event was long forgotten, Phil noticed that Mom and Dad were having trouble finding the time needed to help Phil's younger brother complete a school project. Grabbing the 'bull by the horns,' Phil volunteered to help his brother. He had done the same project in school and felt confident that he could help.

The boys worked well together on the project and when it was complete the younger brother received an excellent grade. Mom and Dad discussed Phil's contribution and decided to reward him for his extra effort. They knocked on the door of his room and came in all smiles, "Phil," they said, "we're real proud of how you helped your brother. We'd like to give you this savings bond as our way of saying thanks." Phil looked at his Mom and Dad and beamed from ear to ear, saying, "Thanks, but I already got my reward." His mother and father looked at him quizzically and asked, "What was that?" And he said, again smiling, "I got personal satisfaction for helping out."

KEY BIBLICAL PRINCIPLES: PERSONAL GROWTH
EMOTIONAL FREEDOM

1. **God offers peace in place of anxiety.**
   Humble yourselves, therefore, under God's mighty hand, that he may lift you up in due time. Cast all your anxiety on him because he cares for you. 1 Peter 5:6-7 (Also Philippians 4:6-7; Isaiah 26:3)

2. **Jesus offers rest for weary souls.**
   Come to me, all who are weary and burdened, and I will give you rest. Take my yoke upon you and learn from me, for I am gentle and humble in heart, and you will find rest for your souls. For my yoke is easy and my burden is light. Matthew 11:28-30

3. **We need not fear for God is with us.**
   So do not fear, for I am with you; do not be dismayed, for I am your God. I will strengthen you and help you; I will uphold you with my righteous right hand. Isaiah 41:10

TRUSTING GOD

1. **Striving in your own strength alone is not profitable.**
   Unless the Lord builds the house, its builders labor in vain. Unless the Lord watches over the city, the watchmen stand guard in vain. In vain you rise early and stay up late, toiling for food to eat, for he grants sleep to those he loves. Psalm 127:1-2

2. **God loves you and He does not want you to be worried about your life and future.**
   Therefore I tell you, do not worry about your life, what you will eat or drink; or about your body, what you will wear. Is not life more important than food, and the body more important than clothes?...Who of you by worrying can add a single hour to his life?...But seek first his kingdom and his righteousness, and all these things will be given to you as well. Therefore do not worry about tomorrow, for tomorrow will worry about itself. Each day has enough trouble of its own. Matthew 6:25, 27, 33-34

PERSONAL DEVELOPMENT

1. **God wants you to guard and develop your mind.**
   Finally, brothers, whatever is true, whatever is noble, whatever is right, whatever is pure, whatever is lovely, whatever is admirable — if anything is excellent or praiseworthy — think about such things. Philippians 4:8

2. **It is wise to learn to control your anger.**
    A quick-tempered man does foolish things, and a crafty man is hated. Proverbs 14:17
    A patient man has great understanding, but a quick-tempered man displays folly. Proverbs 14:29
    A hot-tempered man stirs up dissension, but a patient man calms a quarrel. Proverbs 15:18
    A man's wisdom gives him patience; it is to his glory to overlook an offense. Proverbs 19:11

3. **God wants to renew your mind by the power of the Holy Spirit.**
    Do not conform any longer to the pattern of this world, but be transformed by the renewing of your mind. Then you will be able to test and approve what God's will is — his good, pleasing and perfect will. Romans 12:2 (Also Romans 8:5-9)

4. **God has given you abilities that you should use and develop.**
    Each one should use whatever gift he has received to serve others, faithfully administering God's grace in its various forms. 1 Peter 4:10 (Also 1 Corinthians 12:4-7)

TAKING INVENTORY: PERSONAL GROWTH

LIFE LESSONS

1. Who has provided a positive role model for you in this area of life management?

2. What principles and insights have surfaced from your discussion of this area of life management?

ROLES THAT RELATE TO PERSONAL GROWTH

Roles are functions that you perform, areas in which you have responsibilities or in which you play an important and identifiable part. Examples might include being a student, teacher or a good listener.

1.

2.

3.

DEFINING YOUR LONG-RANGE OBJECTIVE

This statement should be general, non-measurable and non-dated. Summarize your objective for this area of life by completing this statement: "Over the next 5-10 years I want to . . . ."

SPECIFIC GOALS FOR THIS YEAR

Goals are specific, measurable and time-dated. What two or three goals do you want to accomplish this year in the area of personal growth?

1.

2.

3.

DISCIPLINES

What positive routines and helpful habits do you need to continue on a regular basis, daily, weekly, or monthly, that will help you remain focused, orderly and efficient?

1.

2.

3.

4.

VICTORIES

What progress or victories have you experienced so far in your efforts to succeed in growing mentally and emotionally?

CHALLENGES

What challenges are you having in reaching your goals in this area of personal growth?

PHYSICAL

(HEALTH AND FITNESS)

KEY VERSES: 1 CORINTHIANS 6:19-20

"Do you not know that your body is a temple of the Holy Spirit, who is in you, whom you have received from God? You are not your own; you were bought at a price. Therefore honor God with your body."

KEY CONCEPT

God has entrusted each of us with a body. We are responsible to God for how we use and care for our bodies. We must not yield our bodies to the desires of the sinful nature (Galatians 5:16-21). Instead, we must honor God with how we live, for our bodies are the temple of God's Spirit, who dwells within every believer.

LIFE ILLUSTRATION

Carl was just about to complete his last year of high school when the incident occurred. One afternoon, when he was with a group of his friends, one of them brought out a bottle of wine and offered it to Carl. When he declined, they laughed and made fun of him. Carl was hurt.

When he went home that evening, he discussed the matter with his father. They had already talked about the fact that the body is a temple for the Holy Spirit and that it needed to be treated with respect. Carl understood this, but he couldn't reconcile it with the demands of his peer group. His father offered the following explanation by way of a story:

"You know, Carl, when I was your age, something happened that caused me to make a decision. We were just getting ready for the prom, and a couple of evenings before, several of my friends came by in an automobile and offered to drive out to the party scene and look it over. Well, I was just about to get into the car when I noticed that there were several bottles of beer in the back seat, and a couple of the guys had alcohol on their breath.   Despite the fact that they would make fun of me, I said, 'No, I'm just not going to be able to go.' They yelled and screamed at me, and then took off with a hoot and a howl. They were waving their arms and singing with the radio up loud looking like they were going to have the most fun that they'd ever had. Early the next morning, we got the news that the automobile and everyone in it had been destroyed in an accident that evening. You see, Carl, if I hadn't made the right decision, neither you nor I would be here today to talk about it."

Understanding his father's meaning, Carl made the decision to abstain from alcohol, drugs and smoking. Who knows if that had anything to do with Carl convincing his school soccer team to do the same? The team went on that year to win the state championship.

KEY BIBLICAL PRINCIPLES: PHYSICAL
HONORING GOD WITH YOUR BODY

1. **God's Spirit resides within each believer rather than in a temple made with human hands.**
    Do you not know that your body is a temple of the Holy Spirit, who is in you, whom you have received from God? You are not your own; you were bought at a price. Therefore honor God with your body.
    1 Corinthians 6:19-20 (Also see Romans 8:9-11)

2. **You must honor God with your body by avoiding sin and offering your body as an instrument of righteousness.**
    Therefore do not let sin reign in your mortal body so that you obey its evil desires. Do not offer the parts of your body to sin, as instruments of wickedness, but rather offer yourselves to God, as those who have been brought from death to life; and offer the parts of your body to him as instruments of righteousness. Romans 6:12-13
    (Also 2 Corinthians 6:16-7:1)

3. **Your lifestyle needs to be a helpful example to others.**
    *So, whether you eat or drink or whatever you do, do it all for the glory
    of God. Do not cause anyone to stumble, whether Jews, Greeks or
    the church of God.* 1 Corinthians 10:31-32

BALANCING WORK AND REST

1. **Avoid the extremes of being lazy or a workaholic.**
    *The fool folds his hands and ruins himself. Better one handful with
    tranquility than two handfuls with toil and chasing after the wind.*
    Ecclesiastes 4:5-6

2. **God wants you to keep a balance between work and rest.**
    *"Remember the Sabbath day by keeping it holy. Six days you shall
    labor and do all your work, but the seventh day is a Sabbath to the
    Lord your God. On it you shall not do any work, neither you, nor
    your son or daughter, nor your manservant or maidservant, nor your
    animals, nor the alien within your gates."* Exodus 20:8-10
    (Also Mark 2:27)

GOD'S DESIGN FOR HUMAN SEXUALITY

1. **Believers must avoid all sexual immorality.**
    *The body is not meant for sexual immorality, but for the Lord, and the
    Lord for the body.... Flee from sexual immorality. All other sins a
    man commits are outside his body, but he who sins sexually sins
    against his own body.* 1 Corinthians 6:13b-18

2. **Sex should only be experienced and enjoyed by a man and
    woman who have entered into the bonds of marriage.**
    *Marriage should be honored by all, and the marriage bed kept pure, for
    God will judge the adulterer and all the sexually immoral.*
    Hebrews 13:4 (Also 1 Corinthians 7:2-5)

3. **Homosexuality is unnatural, indecent and immoral. It is rebellion against God and results in severe consequences, physically and spiritually.**

   For although they knew God, they neither glorified him as God nor gave thanks to him, but their thinking became futile and their foolish hearts were darkened....Because of this, God gave them over to shameful lusts. Even their women exchanged natural relations for unnatural ones. In the same way the men also abandoned natural relations with women and were inflamed with lust for one another. Romans 1:21, 26-27 (Also see 1 Corinthians 6:9-11)

HUMAN ORIGIN AND DESTINATION

1. **The human body was designed and created by God.**

   And the Lord God formed man from the dust of the ground and breathed into his nostrils the breath of life, and man became a living being. Genesis 2:7 (Also Psalm 139:13-14)

2. **The death of the human body is the result of sin.**

   Therefore, just as sin entered the world through one man, and death through sin, and in this way death came to all men, because all sinned. Romans 5:12

3. **We will be judged for how we have managed our lives and our bodies.**

   For we must all appear before the judgment seat of Christ, that each one may receive what is due him for the things done while in the body, whether good or bad. 2 Corinthians 5:10
   (Also 1 Thessalonians 5:23)

4. **Jesus Christ received a perfect physical body after His resurrection from the grave; likewise, believers have the promise of a glorified physical body in heaven.**

   But Christ has indeed been raised from the dead, the firstfruits of those who have fallen asleep. For since death came through a man, the resurrection of the dead comes also through a man. For as in Adam all die, so in Christ all will be made alive. 1 Corinthians 15:20-22
   (Also Philippians 3:20-21)

TAKING INVENTORY: PHYSICAL

LIFE LESSONS

1. Who has provided a positive role model for you in this area of life management?

2. What principles and insights have surfaced from your discussion of this area of life management?

ROLES THAT RELATE TO HEALTH AND FITNESS

Roles are functions that you perform, areas in which you have responsibilities or in which you play an important and identifiable part. Examples might include being an athlete, meal planner, coach or a personal example of healthy living.

1.

2.

3.

DEFINING YOUR LONG-RANGE OBJECTIVE

This statement should be general, non-measurable and non-dated. Summarize your objective for this area of life by completing this statement: "Over the next 5-10 years I want to . . . ."

SPECIFIC GOALS FOR THIS YEAR
Goals are specific, measurable and time-dated. What two or three goals do you want to accomplish this year in the area of the physical?

1.

2.

3.

DISCIPLINES
What positive routines and helpful habits do you need to continue on a regular basis, daily, weekly, or monthly, that will help you remain focused, orderly and efficient?

1.

2.

3.

4.

VICTORIES
What progress or victories have you experienced so far in your efforts to succeed in your personal health and fitness?

CHALLENGES
What challenges are you having in reaching your health and fitness goals?

SOCIAL

(FRIENDSHIP AND CITIZENSHIP)

KEY VERSES: PHILIPPIANS 2:3-4

"Do nothing out of selfish ambition or vain conceit, but in humility consider others better than yourselves. Each of you should look not only to your own interests, but also to the interests of others."

KEY CONCEPT

God has created mankind as a relational being. We live in relationship to God and to other people. Jesus emphasized the importance of these two relationships when He offered two great commandments: "Love the Lord your God. . . ." and "Love your neighbor as yourself" (Matthew 22:37-39). The Bible affirms the importance of good friends and godly fellowship; however, it also affirms that God's people must play a positive role in meeting the needs of society as well. Christians should not isolate themselves. Instead, they should seek to be Christ's ambassadors to a lost and needy world (2 Corinthians 5:17-21).

LIFE ILLUSTRATION

Many years ago, there was a wall that had been constructed between East and West Germany. One evening, the people who were on the west side of the wall called out to those on the east side. They spoke of the harmony, peace, and brotherhood that they experienced living under the political system in the west. The folks on the east side in turn jeered at them, "Your leaders are so weak that they must have their citizens come to the wall and beg peace from us." To show their disdain for the westerners, the people on the east side gathered all their garbage and threw it over the wall as an offering and response to the appeals of those on the west side.

The next morning, when the westerners went to the wall and saw the trash and refuse, they shook their heads in disbelief and cleaned it up. Later that afternoon they had a meeting.

A week later, the people on the east side of the wall were amazed to find that the night before, a lot of work had been done on the part of the westerners. For there on the east side were packages containing gifts of books, radios, clothing, and food as presents for the people on the east side. Among the gifts was a note which was meant to appeal to the leaders of the easterners, and it said simply, "We need each other to survive. Love thy neighbor as thyself."

Many months later, people on the east and west side of that wall joined in prayer along with brothers and sisters around the world. The rest is history. The wall between family members, the wall that had represented the separation of legitimate authority from illegitimate authority, disappeared in a breath, overnight. Today, we enjoy the benefits of a united Germany and are moving towards the benefits of a united world.

KEY BIBLICAL PRINCIPLES: SOCIAL

CHRISTIAN FELLOWSHIP AND LOVE

1. **Unity and love are the marks of Christians.**
    "A new commandment I give you: Love one another. As I have loved you, so you must love one another. All men will know that you are my disciples if you love one another." John 13:34-35; 17:23
    (Also see Romans 15:5-6)

2. **Christians need to demonstrate mutual concern.**
    Be devoted to one another in brotherly love. Honor one another above yourselves. Romans 12:10 (Also 1 Corinthians 12:26; Galatians 6:2)

3. **Christians are to remember and serve those in need.**
    Remember those in prison as if you were their fellow prisoners, and those who are mistreated as if you yourselves were suffering....And do not forget to do good and to share with others, for with such sacrifices God is pleased. Hebrews 13:3, 16

CITIZENSHIP

1. **Christians are to submit to legitimate authority and demonstrate good citizenship as a witness for Christ.**
    Everyone must submit himself to the governing authorities, for there is no authority except that which God has established. The authorities that exist have been established by God. Romans 13:1 (Also see Romans 13:2-7; 1 Peter 2:12-14)

2. **Endeavor to maintain good relationships with everyone.**
    If it is possible, as far as it depends on you, live at peace with everyone. Romans 12:18

3. **God calls us to pray for our political leaders and those in authority over us.**
    I urge, then, first of all, that requests, prayers, intercession and thanksgiving be made for everyone — for kings and all those in authority, that we may live peaceful and quiet lives in all godliness and holiness. This is good, and pleases God our Savior, who wants all men to be saved and to come to a knowledge of the truth. 1 Timothy 2:1-4 (Also see Proverbs 21:1)

FRIENDSHIPS

1. **Friends are treasures in times of trouble.**
    A friend loves at all times, and a brother is born for adversity. Proverbs 17:17

2. **Choose friends that do not ask you to compromise your loyalty and obedience to God.**
    Peter and the other apostles replied: "We must obey God rather than men!" Acts 5:29 (Also see Galatians 1:10)

3. **We need the help of other people to succeed in life.**
    Two are better than one, because they have a good return for their work: If one falls down, his friend can help him up. But pity the man who falls and has no one to help him up! Also, if two lie down together, they will keep warm. But how can one keep warm alone? Ecclesiastes 4:9-12

SOCIAL CONCERN

1. **Christians must be concerned about justice for the poor.**
   The righteous care about justice for the poor, but the wicked have no such concern. Proverbs 29:7 (Also see Galatians 2:10)

2. **You must seek to fulfill the second greatest commandment, to love your neighbor as yourself.**
   "And the second is like it: 'Love your neighbor as yourself.' All the Law and the Prophets hang on these two commandments." Matthew 22:39-40

3. **Your life as a believer must be marked by an attitude of service to the needs and interests of others.**
   Jesus called them together and said, "You know that those who are regarded as rulers of the Gentiles lord it over them, and their high officials exercise authority over them. Not so with you. Instead, whoever wants to become great among you must be your servant, and whoever wants to be first must be slave of all. For even the Son of Man did not come to be served, but to serve, and to give his life as a ransom for many." Mark 10:42-45

TAKING INVENTORY: SOCIAL

LIFE LESSONS

1. Who has provided a positive role model for you in this area of life management?

2. What principles and insights have surfaced from your discussion of this area of life management?

ROLES THAT RELATE TO FRIENDSHIP AND CITIZENSHIP

Roles are functions that you perform, areas in which you have responsibilities or in which you play an important and identifiable part. Examples might include being a best friend, a model of citizenship, a neighbor or a political worker.

1.

2.

3.

DEFINING YOUR LONG-RANGE OBJECTIVE

This statement should be general, non-measurable and non-dated. Summarize your objective for this area of life by completing this statement: "Over the next 5-10 years I want to . . . ."

SPECIFIC GOALS FOR THIS YEAR

Goals are specific, measurable and time-dated. What two or three social goals do you want to accomplish this year?

1.

2.

3.

DISCIPLINES

What positive routines and helpful habits do you need to continue on a regular basis, daily, weekly, or monthly, that will help you remain focused, orderly and efficient?

1.

2.

3.

4.

VICTORIES

What progress or victories have you experienced so far in your efforts to succeed as a friend and citizen?

CHALLENGES

What challenges are you having in reaching your social goals?

SPIRITUAL

(SEEKING AND SERVING GOD)

KEY VERSE: GALATIANS 2:20

"I have been crucified with Christ and I no longer live, but Christ
lives in me. The life I live in the body, I live by faith in the Son of
God, who loved me and gave himself up for me."

KEY CONCEPT

You have been created in God's image (Genesis 5:1-2) and He desires
fellowship with you (John 17:20-26). Being alive spiritually requires
submission to Jesus Christ and a death to self-will (Galatians 2:20).
Jesus clearly stated in John 14:6, "I am the way and the truth and the
life." To nurture your spiritual life requires seeking God through an
abiding relationship with Jesus Christ and serving Him through a willing obedience to His commands (John 15:1-17).

LIFE ILLUSTRATION

James S. Hewett relates the following experience on a flight from
Denver to Wichita. The last traveler to board was a paralyzed man
being carried on and seated by flight attendants. He was strapped in
tightly, but as the pilot taxied to the runway the movement of the air-
plane caused him to fall to his right. The stewardess again propped
him up and we were airborne. Beverages were served, then a meal.
As I finished the meal, I looked up to see the paralyzed gentleman,
probably 27 years old, with the meal before him with no one to feed
him. My eyes filled with tears. The hostesses were busy serving food
to all the passengers, but here was a person traveling alone who could
only look at the meal. It was beautifully prepared, tasty, and far above
average for airline food.

Before I could wipe the tears from my eyes, I slipped from my seat to
his side and inquired if the stewardess would be helping him eat. He

did not know. I asked if I might help him. He responded with "Oh, thank you, I would be so grateful for your help." As I cut the meal into bite sizes and placed them in his mouth, I felt awkward, conspicuous, but much needed. Before long I was coordinating bites as well as if they were entering my own mouth. He told me of his unfortunate accident, his lonesomeness, his joys, his struggles, his faith, his hope. His name was Bill. Our spirits blended — we experienced sacrament! Upon returning to my seat, my spirit was humbled as I thought of all the people who have had the Good News of the gospel set before them. It's available but no one to feed them, crippled with spiritual and psychological paralysis — and no one to feed them. My spirit flowed to the words Jesus asked Peter, "Do you love me?" Jesus responded, "Feed my sheep."

KEY BIBLICAL PRINCIPLES: SPIRITUAL

SEEKING GOD

1. **God desires your complete and total commitment.**
    Therefore, I urge you, brothers, in view of God's mercy, to offer your bodies as living sacrifices, holy and pleasing to God — this is your spiritual act of worship. Do not conform any longer to the pattern of this world, but be transformed by the renewing of your mind. Then you will be able to test and approve what God's will is — his good, pleasing and perfect will. Romans 12:1-2

2. **You must seek to fulfill the greatest commandment, to love the Lord your God with all your being.**
    "Teacher, which is the greatest commandment in the Law?" Jesus replied: " 'Love the Lord your God with all your heart and with all your soul and with all your mind.' This is the first and greatest commandment. And the second is like it: 'Love your neighbor as yourself.' All the Law and the Prophets hang on these two commandments." Matthew 22:36-40

3. **You need to maintain regular times of worship and fellowship with other Christians.**
   And let us consider how we may spur one another on toward love and good deeds. Let us not give up meeting together, as some are in the habit of doing, but let us encourage one another and all the more as you see the Day approaching. Hebrew 10:24-25

   They devoted themselves to the apostles' teaching and to the fellowship, to the breaking of bread and to prayer. Acts 2:42

4. **Your hope and trust must be found in God rather than your own resources.**
   Now faith is being sure of what we hope for and certain of what we do not see. And without faith it is impossible to please God, because any one who comes to him must believe that he exists and that he rewards those who earnestly seek him. Hebrews 11:1, 6

SERVING GOD

1. **You are Christ's ambassador to your world.**
   We are therefore Christ's ambassadors, as though God were making his appeal through us. We implore you on Christ's behalf: Be reconciled to God. God made him who had no sin to be sin for us, so that in him we might become the righteousness of God. 2 Corinthians 5:20-21

2. **All followers of Christ are to participate in the great commission.**
   "Therefore go and make disciples of all nations, baptizing them in the name of the Father and of the Son and of the Holy Spirit, and teaching them to obey everything I have commanded you. And surely I will be with you always, to the very end of the age." Matthew 28:19-20

3. **Christians are to be "salt" and "light" to a lost world.**
   "You are the salt of the earth. But if the salt loses its saltiness, how can it be made salty again? It is no longer good for anything, except to be thrown out and trampled by men. You are the light of the world. A city on a hill cannot be hidden. Neither do people light a lamp and put it under a bowl. Instead they put it on its stand, and it gives light to

everyone in the house. In the same way, let your light shine before men, that they may see your good deeds and praise your Father in heaven." Matthew 5:13-16

4. **God has given you spiritual gifts that you are to use to His glory and for the benefit of others.**
We have different gifts, according to the grace given us. If a man's gift is prophesying, let him use it in proportion to his faith. If it is serving, let him serve; if it is teaching, let him teach; if it is encouraging, let him encourage; if it is contributing to the needs of others, let him give generously; if it is leadership, let him govern diligently; if it is showing mercy, let him do it cheerfully. Romans 12:6-8

5. **Serving God also means helping those in need.**
If anyone has material possessions and sees his brother in need but has no pity on him, how can the love of God be in him? 1 John 3:17

TAKING INVENTORY: SPIRITUAL

LIFE LESSONS

1. Who has provided a positive role model for your spiritual life?

2. What principles and insights have surfaced from your discussion of this area of life management?

ROLES THAT RELATE TO YOUR SPIRITUAL LIFE

Roles are functions that you perform, areas in which you have responsibilities or in which you play an important and identifiable part. Examples include being a Christian, a disciple, and an ambassador for Christ.

1.

2.

3.

DEFINING YOUR LONG-RANGE OBJECTIVE

This statement should be general, non-measurable and non-dated. Summarize your objective for this area of life by completing this statement: "Over the next 5-10 years I want to . . . ."

SPECIFIC GOALS FOR THIS YEAR

Goals are specific, measurable and time-dated. What two or three goals do you want to accomplish this year in the area of spiritual life?

1.

2.

3.

DISCIPLINES

What positive routines and helpful habits do you need to continue on
a regular basis, daily, weekly, or monthly, that will help you remain
focused, orderly and efficient?

1.

2.

3.

4.

VICTORIES

What progress or victories have you experienced so far in your efforts
to succeed in your spiritual life?

CHALLENGES

What challenges are you having in reaching your spiritual goals?

WORK

(Personal Contribution)

KEY VERSE: COLOSSIANS 3:17

"And whatever you do, whether in word or deed, do it all in the name of the Lord Jesus, giving thanks to God the Father through him."

KEY CONCEPT

Work (personal productivity) is an honorable part of God's plan for everyone (Genesis 2:15). Making a personal contribution in life is fulfilling and meaningful. God has uniquely gifted each person with the ability to honor Him and help others through their work. It is important to remember that when we demonstrate faithfulness in our work we should do so as an act of worship to God.

LIFE ILLUSTRATION

Ramey was the old physician — in fact, the only physician that the town ever had. Ramey often would slip out in the middle of the afternoon to go fishing when the season was right because he loved his bass. His patients and the townspeople all knew that Ramey did this, and they forgave his indulgence. Almost everyone had a story they could tell which justified their forgiveness. There was Bob, whose wife's life had been saved one evening by an emergency appendectomy in their home. Then there was Luke, whose daughter's tonsils had been removed one evening when they had become so swollen that she could hardly breathe, let alone eat. And, then there was little Tommy, who owed his very life to the doctor. In the middle of the evening, when their station wagon had broken down, Dr. Ramey came and assisted in the birth of Tommy because they couldn't get to the hospital.

Old Mose was the janitor at the local school. He was in his 75th year and, like the doctor, was known and loved by everyone there. The old janitor, Mose, gave as much of his life to the earnest pursuit of his duties as did Dr. Ramey. They both were blessed with doing something that they loved to do as an expression of love to the people around them whom they served. They were faithful in their tasks and unique in their abilities.

Mose and Ramey passed away on the same day. They never really knew each other well, but they knew each other by reputation. The Great Equalizer had claimed them together, and their passing was marked by a turnout of the entire town. It seemed that everyone who had attended the service had come to see both of them. Whether it was the doctor or the old janitor, one had affected every member of that community in his own special way through the work that he had done and the love that he had expressed.

KEY BIBLICAL PRINCIPLES: WORK

YOUR WORK IS MEANINGFUL

1. **Work is a gift to us from God.**
   What does the worker gain from his toil? I have seen the burden God has laid on men. He has made everything beautiful in its time. He has also set eternity in the hearts of men; yet they cannot fathom what God has done from beginning to end. I know that there is nothing better for men than to be happy and do good while they live. That every man may eat and drink, and find satisfaction in all his toil — this is the gift of God. Ecclesiastes 3:9-13

2. **God created mankind in His image as a worker prior to the Fall.**
   Then God said, "Let us make man in our image, in our likeness, and let them rule over the fish of the sea and the birds of the air, over the livestock, over all the earth, and over all the creatures that move along the ground." So God created man in his own image, in the image of God he created him; male and female he created them. God blessed them and said to them, "Be fruitful and increase in number; fill the earth and subdue it. Rule over the fish of the sea and the birds of the air and over every living creature that moves on the ground." Then

God said, "I give you every seed-bearing plant on the face of the whole earth and every tree that has fruit with seed in it. They will be yours for food." Genesis 1:26-29

The Lord God took man and put him in the Garden of Eden to work it and take care of it. Genesis 2:15

YOUR WORK CAN HONOR GOD

1. Work provides a means for obedience to Jesus' two great commandments: Love God and love other people.
    "Teacher, which is the greatest commandment in the Law?" Jesus replied: " 'Love the Lord your God with all your heart and with all your soul and with all your mind.' This is the first and greatest commandment. And the second is like it: 'Love your neighbor as yourself.' All the Law and Prophets hang on these two commandments." Matthew 22:36-40

2. Your work is an act of worship. Whether employer or employee, you must work with the realization that it is God who evaluates and rewards your efforts.
    Whatever you do, work at it with all your heart, as working for the Lord, not for men, since you know that you will receive an inheritance from the Lord as a reward. It is the Lord Christ you are serving. Anyone who does wrong will be repaid for his wrong, and there is no favoritism. Masters, provide your slaves with what is right and fair, because you know that you also have a Master in heaven. Colossians 3:23-4:1 (Also see Ephesians 6:5-9, Titus 2:9,10)

3. You must work in order to fulfill your financial commitments and avoid being a burden on society.
    Make it your ambition to lead a quiet life, to mind your own business and to work with your hands, just as we told you, so that your daily life may win the respect of outsiders and so that you will not be dependent on anybody. 1 Thessalonians 4:11-12 (Also see 2 Thessalonians 3:6-15)

YOU OFFER A UNIQUE PERSONAL CONTRIBUTION

1. **God knows you personally and has a plan for you.**
    *"For I know the plans I have for you," declares the Lord, "plans to
    prosper you and not to harm you, plans to give you hope and a future.
    Then you will call upon me and come and pray to me, and I will listen
    to you. You will seek me and find me when you seek me with all of
    your heart."* Jeremiah 29:11-13 (Also see Acts 13:1-5)

2. **God designed you with certain talents, abilities and interests;
    the way He designed you offers clues to the types of service
    available for you to perform in His world.**
    *There are different kinds of gifts, but the same Spirit. There are
    different kinds of service, but the same Lord. There are different kinds
    of working, but the same God works all of them in all men.*
    1 Corinthians 12:4-7

    *Each one should use whatever gift he has received to serve others,
    faithfully administering God's grace in its various forms.* 1 Peter 4:10
    (Also see Psalm 139:13-16)

TAKING INVENTORY: WORK

LIFE LESSONS

1. Who has provided a positive role model for you in this area of life
    management?

2. What principles and insights have surfaced from your discussion
    of this area of life management?

ROLES THAT RELATE TO YOUR WORK

Roles are functions that you perform, areas in which you have responsibilities or in which you play an important and identifiable part. Examples of work roles might include various responsibilities relating to your employment: manager, employer, customer service or sales representative. However, your personal contributions may not translate into income: homemaker, volunteer teacher's aid, community health volunteer or lay pastor in a local church.

1.

2.

3.

4.

DEFINING YOUR LONG-RANGE OBJECTIVES

These statements should be general, non-measurable and non-dated. Since your work may involve several roles or areas of responsibility, you will likely have more than one long-range objective. Summarize your personal contribution objectives by completing this statement: "Over the next 5-10 years I want to . . . ."

1.

2.

3.

4.

SPECIFIC GOALS FOR THIS YEAR

Goals are specific, measurable and time-dated. You may find that you have one, two or three goals for each objective listed above.

1.

2.

3.

4.

5.

6.

DISCIPLINES

What positive routines and helpful habits do you need to continue on a regular basis, daily, weekly, or monthly, that will help you remain focused, orderly and efficient?

1.

2.

3.

4.

VICTORIES

What progress or victories have you experienced so far in your efforts to succeed in your work?

CHALLENGES

What challenges are you having in reaching your work goals?

BALANCING LIFE'S DEMANDS

KEY VERSE: 1 CORINTHIANS 10:31

"So whether you eat or drink or whatever you do, do it all for the glory of God."

KEY CONCEPT

Balancing life's demands begins by acknowledging that God is the one who deserves our loyalty, love, service and devotion. We are stewards of the gift of life which He has given. We have nothing that has not come from His hand. Therefore, we must seek to honor God in all areas of life. Time is the context in which we must seek to balance these demands of life. Therefore, how we manage our time is of great importance, for time is life. Our focus here is not so much about being efficient (doing things right), but being effective (doing the right things).

LIFE ILLUSTRATION

Most people are familiar with a triathlon or a decathlon, but balancing life's demands can more easily be illustrated by the lesser known pentathlon. The triathlon tests athletic endurance through a three-event competition which includes riding a bike 24 miles, swimming about one mile and running a race of about six miles. The decathlon tests athletic skill and strength using 10 track and field events. However, the modern pentathlon is a five-event Olympic contest which includes a 5,000 meter cross-country horseback ride, a 4,000 meter cross-country run, a 300 meter swim, foil fencing and pistol shooting.

Can you imagine entering a contest where you had to compete with skill in all five of these areas? Perhaps you are a good runner, but how are you at sword fighting? Perhaps you can swim well, but can you ride a horse or shoot a pistol with accuracy? In order to win the pentathlon you must do well enough in each event to receive the highest combined total of points.

Balancing the seven areas of life management can seem as difficult as winning a pentathlon. Everyone is good in one or more of the areas of life management: family, finances, personal growth, physical, social, spiritual and work. But to win the contest requires a good score in all seven areas. Those who focus on succeeding in only one or two areas neglect other areas where they must do well in order to win in life. You can have a successful career but lose your spouse and children. Or consider what Jesus said about financial success at the expense of your spiritual life, "What good will it be for a man if he gains the whole world, yet forfeits his soul? Or what can a man give in exchange for his soul?" (Matthew 16:26)

Life is like a pentathlon. It requires that each of us develop skills in very diverse areas. We must do well in areas in which we have strengths and in areas where we have weaknesses. We must realize that true success involves a balancing of life's demands.

KEY PRINCIPLES: BALANCED LIVING

STEP 1: GIVE GOD FIRST PLACE IN YOUR LIFE

1. **What is the center for your life?** This center is the controlling focus that directs your life. For some it is money, self, career, friends, family or health. What have been some of the things that have been your center in the past? What is it now?

2. How does life become "out-of-balance" when any one of the seven areas of life management becomes your center, the controlling focus of your life?

3. Balancing life begins by making God the center, the controlling focus of your life. We are stewards of the life that God has given us. In everything we do, we should consider it an act of service to God. How have you sought to honor and glorify God in each of the seven areas? Read 1 Corinthians 10:31.

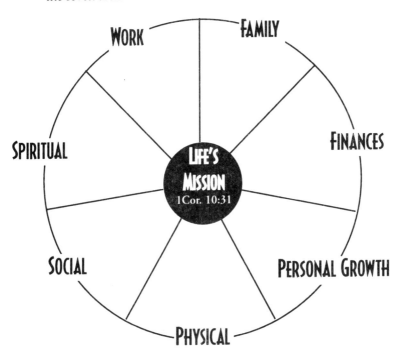

4. **All the areas of life are interrelated.** A choice or action in one area will have an effect on all the others. Balance in life does not mean that you spend equal amounts of time in each area of life management. Given 100 hours during one week, how much time would you spend in each of the following areas if you were to reflect a balanced life?

    _____Family (marriage and children)
    _____Finances (sharing, spending, saving)
    _____Personal Growth (mental & emotional)
    _____Physical (health and fitness)
    _____Social (friendship and citizenship)
    _____Spiritual (seeking and serving God)
    _____Work (personal contribution)

STEP 2: DISCOVER GOD'S PURPOSE FOR YOU

1. **Take a look at what you've got.** (Possessions, pages 19-24).
   Thank God for all that He has entrusted to you. Begin to serve
   Him with what you have and He will direct your life. How are
   you trying to use your possessions to their greatest effectiveness in
   serving God?

2. **Review your life Purpose.** (Purpose, pages 25-30)

   a. **Biblical Purposes.** What do you know to be God's will
      for all Christians as revealed in the Bible?

   b. **Personal Priorities.** What personal priorities are at the
      top of your list?

   c. **Personal Passion.** Review your personal mission
      statement from page 30 and write it below or update it.

STEP 3: SET MEASURABLE GOALS FOR EACH AREA

Once a year evaluate and reaffirm your purpose statement. Then write
three to five goals for the year in each of the seven areas of life management. Share these goals with your mentor. The area of Work will
often have a greater number of goals listed because of numerous areas
of responsibility and focus. How is it helpful to limit the number of
yearly goals for each of the seven areas?

STEP 4: MAKE THE CALENDAR YOUR FRIEND

1. **Find a calendar that works for you.** Everyone needs a way of
   recording the appointments and commitments of life. Some can
   manage with a simple monthly calendar while others need a

detailed diary page for every day. Make sure your goals are measurable by writing them into your annual calendar. Do you have a calendar that works for you? How do you use it?

2. **Work your calendar.** If your calendar and your budget do not reflect your goals, then your goals are merely wishes. If you do not take control of your calendar, others will. Plan ahead, asking God how He wants you to invest the time that He has entrusted to you.

    a. First, write into your calendar all known personal and family commitments for the next 12 months.

    b. Second, make the calendar your friend by reviewing your goals and writing them into your 12-month calendar. Include personal days, vacations, weekly dates, family nights, one- or two-day getaways, etc. Think about it — in the past, have you scheduled the time needed to fulfill your goals?

3. **Establish a standard weekly schedule.** The disciplines that are needed to sustain a balanced life can best be set into the context of a standard weekly schedule. This is a log of the helpful habits and positive routines that keep you on track and make life less confusing. A standard weekly schedule keeps you from having to decide each day just what you are to do. You may never actually follow the schedule in every detail, but it serves as a guide, reminding you of the disciplines that bring order and balance to your lives. Disciplines include: work, rest, exercise, study, worship, recreation, family time, etc. What does your standard week consist of at this time?

STANDARD WEEKLY SCHEDULE

(See Example, Appendix C)

	SUN	MON	TUE	WED	THU	FRI	SAT
BREAKFAST							
WORK							
LUNCH							
WORK							
AFTER WORK							
DINNER							
AFTER DINNER							
LATE NIGHT							
LATE NIGHT 2							

STEP 5: PRIORITIZE YOUR "TO DO LIST"

Everyone knows what a "TO DO LIST" is, even if they just keep it in their mind. However, just because you write something on that list doesn't mean it is really important or that you should even be the one to do it. Many things get on your list that are "urgent" but not "important" and many "important" things may never even make your "list." Consider the following plan for determining which items you will include on your "TO DO LIST."

1. Begin by establishing your goals for the year. Set three to five goals for each of the seven areas of life management. You may wish to prioritize your annual goals by labeling them:

    > A = Must Do
    > B = Should Do
    > C = Nice To Do
    > D = Delegate

2. At the beginning of each month review all of your annual goals and decide which ones you will work on that month. Again, you may wish to prioritize these monthly goals using the ABCD method.

3. In preparation for each week, review your monthly goals in light of your weekly schedule. Make a weekly "TO DO LIST" which reflects progress toward your monthly goals.

4. In preparation for each day, review your weekly goals and create a daily "TO DO LIST." You may wish to prioritize your daily list by placing the numbers one through five by the most important items. Start with item number one, then move to number two and so on until you have completed the list or run out of time. Items of lesser importance may have to be handled the following day.

MENTORING CHECKLIST

(SAMPLE SESSION)

Plan to meet with your mentor on a regular basis. Begin by meeting monthly. This checklist should be used to prepare yourself to meet with your mentor.[1] Your discussion can involve any of the Seven Areas of Life Management.

SPECIFIC GOALS FOR THIS MONTH

Goals are specific and measurable. What are the top two or three goals you want to accomplish this month? (list in the order of priority)

1.

2.

3.

DECISIONS

What upcoming decisions do you need to make in relation to these goals?

PROBLEMS

What problems are you having in reaching your goals?

PLANS
What plans are you implementing in order to accomplish your goals?

VICTORIES
What progress or victories have you experienced so far in your efforts?

PRAYER REQUESTS
What should we pray about today that would make a difference for you?

OTHER CHALLENGES
Are there any personal roadblocks, blind spots, or fears that you would like to discuss?

APPENDIX A

EXAMPLES: PERSONAL MISSION STATEMENTS

David Durey:

"I am dedicated to equipping and mobilizing church members for the work of ministry in fulfilling the great commission."

EQUIPPING, MOBILIZING CHRISTIANS

Dr. Chuck Goldberg:

HELP PEOPLE FLOURISH

APPENDIX B
EXAMPLES: SEVEN AREAS OF LIFE MANAGEMENT

FAMILY (MARRIAGE AND CHILDREN)

Roles:
1. Husband
2. Father
3. Son and brother

Long-range objective: "Over the next 5-10 years I want to. . ."

Build a strong marriage relationship; raise children into personal maturity and faith in Christ.

Disciplines (daily, weekly, monthly and on-going):
1. Weekly date with my wife.
2. Weekly family night.
3. Daily dinner meal as a family.
4. Day off (family time 1/3 of day).
5. 1-1 for each child with each parent 1X monthly.

This Year's Goals:
1. 5 get away overnight trips alone with my wife.
2. 1 get away with each child this summer.
3. Family camping and WA. vacation.
4. Get a dog for the children.

FINANCIAL (SHARING, SPENDING, SAVING)

Roles:
1. Provider
2. Employer
3. Primary manager of family finances

Long-range objective: "Over the next 5-10 years I want to. . ."

Provide for family needs within a modest lifestyle; limit expenses to maximize giving, savings for retirement, emergency, and opportunity.

Disciplines (daily, weekly, monthly and on-going):
1. Pay myself first. Save for emergency fund and investments.
2. Keep a personal budget up to date each month.
3. Acknowledge God's provision by tithing to my church.
4. Give to the needs of others.

This Year's Goals:
1. Establish a home based family business.
2. Contingency Fund equal to six months income.
3. Housing improvements: Finish dining area; finish bathrooms, fence completed, paint kitchen.

PERSONAL GROWTH (MENTAL AND EMOTIONAL)

Roles:
1. Student
2. Creative Thinker
3. Teacher

Long-range objective: "Over the next 5-10 years I want to . . ."

Continually learn and grow; seek to maximize my gifts, talents and ministry skills and those of my family; remain emotionally balanced and relaxed.

Disciplines (daily, weekly, monthly and on-going):
1. Time alone each week (personal play/relax time).
2. Regular reading for personal and professional growth.
3. Read for pleasure.
4. Regular voice rehearsal.

This Year's Goals:
1. Read 8 - 12 books (1 book a month).
2. Piano lessons for both children.
3. My wife submit writing to publishers of children's literature.

PHYSICAL (HEALTH AND FITNESS)

Roles:
1. Example of healthy living
2. Steward of my body
3. Athlete

Long-range objective: "Over the next 5-10 years I want to. . ."

Maintain physical health and conditioning.

Disciplines (daily, weekly, monthly and on-going):
1. Regular exercise (3X weekly).
2. Eat right/sleep right.

This Year's Goals:
1. Racquetball: Play in a tournament.
2. Swim lessons for both children (2 months).
3. My wife's goal to exercise 4-5X weekly.
4. Two sports each year for both children.

SOCIAL (FRIENDSHIPS AND CITIZENSHIP)

Roles:
1. Citizen
2. Neighbor
3. Friend

Long-range objective: "Over the next 5-10 years I want to. . ."

Keep a balanced relational involvement between family, church, and unchurched friends and neighbors.

Disciplines (daily, weekly, monthly and on-going):
1. Maintain an active involvement in the community.
2. Interact with my neighbors each week.
3. Keep in touch with friends from our past.

This Year's Goals:
1. Develop 2 new couple friendships.
2. Develop 2 peer friendships for myself and my wife.
3. Establish 2 relationships with neighbors or families from children's sports activities.

SPIRITUAL (SEEKING AND SERVING GOD)

Roles:
1. A Christian
2. An ambassador for Christ
3. Discipler and mentor

Long-range objective: "Over the next 5-10 years I want to. . ."

Continually develop a personal relationship with God; remain personally involved in ministry and provide the same for my family.

Disciplines (daily, weekly, monthly and on-going):
1. Spend time alone each day in prayer and Bible reading.
2. Attend a Sunday worship celebration service each week.
3. Participate in a weekly small group meeting.
4. Mentor men.
5. Constantly sow God's message of love and salvation.

This Year's Goals:
1. New Testament Bible Study (6 Books using Biblelog).
2. My wife teach at Women's Bible Study.
3. Family Scripture memory (12 Bible passages).
4. Character development activities for children
    (Scouting, Awanas,etc.).

WORK (PERSONAL CONTRIBUTION) - DR. GOLDBERG

Roles:
1. Medical Doctor
2. Businessman
3. Volunteer Pastor

Long-range objective: "Over the next 5-10 years I want to. . ."
1. Medical: Create a full patient care facility which seeks to help patients understand God's will for their health.
2. Business: Create the largest forum for reaching people in business for the Lord Jesus Christ.
3. Volunteer Pastor: Create a context where I have the time and means to volunteer weekly in Pastoral ministry.

Disciplines (daily, weekly, monthly and on-going):
1. Real-time computerized charting at medical office.
2. Develop algorithm for any disease I've seen more than three times.
3. Make six new business contacts per week.
4. Develop leadership in six or more businesses.
5. Supervise small groups and leaders in my area of ministry.
6. Maintain at least three 1-1 discipling per week.

This Year's Goals:
1. Computerize office fully.
2. Establish protocols for nursing care by phone.
3. Achieve the next level of volume in my business.
4. Develop "Internet" skills
5. Create a strong "Regional Pastor" ministry in my area.

WORK (PERSONAL CONTRIBUTION) - PASTOR DUREY

Roles:
1. District Pastor - small groups, Lay Pastors & discipleship
2. Performing arts
3. Marriage Ministries Pastor
4. Leadership Development Coordinator

Long-range objective: "Over the next 5-10 years I want to help people make a . . ."
1. COMMITMENT TO CHRIST (evangelism) We want people to receive Jesus Christ and experience forgiveness and new life in Him.
2. COMMITMENT TO SPIRITUAL GROWTH (discipleship) We want Christians to become established and grow to maturity in their faith.
3. COMMITMENT TO MINISTRY (equipping to serve) We want Christians to serve God by serving others with the gifts and talents God has given them.
4. COMMITMENT TO SERVANT LEADERSHIP (leadership development) We want to develop leaders of leaders who will impact our city and world for Christ.

Disciplines (daily, weekly, monthly and on-going):
1. Daily Prayer
2. Personal outreach and evangelism
3. Discipling
4. Mentoring
5. Equipping Lay Pastors
6. Personal study
7. Recruiting new leaders

This Year's Goals:
1. Protocol for Pastoral Care
2. Easter Drama: role of Christ
3. Spring Marriage Retreat (40 couples)
4. Six "PREP" marriage classes offered
5. Establish 6 new small groups
6. Recruit 10 new group leaders
7. Create a book for Equipping Lay Pastors

APPENDIX C

EXAMPLE: STANDARD WEEKLY SCHEDULE
DR. CHUCK GOLBERG

	SUN	MON	TUE	WED	THU	FRI	SAT
BREAKFAST							
WORK							
LUNCH							
WORK							
AFTER WORK							
DINNER							
AFTER DINNER							
LATE NIGHT							
LATE NIGHT 2							

EXAMPLE: STANDARD WEEKLY SCHEDULE
DAVID DUREY

SUN	Church	→	Family	→	L.I.F.T. / Family Devotional
MON	Prayer / Date Child / Fitness / Office / Work	Writing	→	Dinner with the family.	Family Activity Night
TUE	Prayer / Fitness / Staff Mtg	→	Appointments		Supervise Groups
WED	Prayer / 1-1 Discipleship / 1-1 Mentoring / Appointments	Music Rehearsal 1:30-2:30 p.m.			Marriage Classes
THU	Prayer / Men's Group / 1-1 Mentoring / Calls/Visits / Fitness	Office			Music Rehearsal / Calls/appointments
FRI	Prayer / Fitness / Study Day	→			Date Night
SAT	Home	Open			Open

APPENDIX D

ONE-TO-ONE MENTORING

Commitment to
SERVANT LEADERSHIP
Commitment to **MINISTRY**
Commitment to **SPIRITUAL GROWTH**
Commitment to **CHRIST**

LEADERSHIP DEVELOPMENT is a by-product of one-to-one relation-ships. As you disciple new and growing followers of Jesus Christ, you will identify those in whom you will want to invest more time. You may find that they desire to be equipped to minister for Christ. You may also recognize that the disciple is one who would work well with you in a mentor-protégé relationship. Each level of one-to-one men-toring fits a specific objective listed below:

COMMITMENT TO CHRIST:
We want people to receive Jesus Christ and experience forgiveness and new life in Him.
Phase One - Winning the Lost:
Friendship evangelism
Intercessory Prayer for friends and neighbors
Acts of Love and deeds of kindness
Initiative events and outreach

COMMITMENT TO SPIRITUAL GROWTH:

We want Christians to become established and grow to maturity in their faith.

Phase Two - Teaching a Disciple:
Steps Toward Spiritual Growth

COMMITMENT TO MINISTRY:

We want Christians to serve God by serving others with the gifts and talents God has given them.

Phase Three - Equipping for Ministry:
Steps Toward Ministry
Lay Pastor Apprentice
Lay Pastor
Lay Pastor Trainer

COMMITMENT TO SERVANT LEADERSHIP:

We want to develop leaders of leaders who will impact our city and world for Christ.

Phase Four - Mentoring a Protégé:
Part I.   Mentoring for Effective Living
                Steps Toward Balancing Life's Demands
Part II. Volunteer & Vocational Ministry Staff
                Lay Pastor Leader
                Ministry Director
                Assistant Pastor
                Associate Pastor or District Pastor

NOTES

INTRODUCTION

1. Bobb Biehl, *Mentoring: Confidence in Finding a Mentor and Becoming One* (Nashville, TN: Broadman and Holman Publishers, 1996), 19.
2. Paul D. Stanley and J. Robert Clinton, *Connecting: The Mentoring Relationships You Need to Succeed in Life* (Colorado Springs, CO: NavPress, 1992), 38. Used by permission of NavPress, for copies call 1-800-366-7788.
3. Bobb Biehl, Jerry "Chip" MacGregor and Glen Urquhart, *Mentoring, How to Find a Mentor and How to Become One* (Lake Mary, FL: Masterplanning Group International, 1994), 2. This 20-page booklet provides an excellent introduction to the basics of mentoring. This booklet and additional mentoring resources are available through Masterplanning Group International, Box 952499, Lake Mary, Florida 32795-2499, Telephone (407) 330-2028, (800) 443-1976.
4. Paul D. Stanley and J. Robert Clinton, *Connecting: The Mentoring Relationships You Need to Succeed in Life* (Colorado Springs, CO: NavPress, 1992), 42. Used by permission of NavPress, for copies call 1-800-366-7788.
5. Bobb Biehl, *Increasing Your Leadership Confidence* (Sisters, OR: Questar Publishers, 1989), 36. In our personal struggles to gain balance in our own lives we have sought to give definition to the various categories of life. Years ago, our mentors introduced us to *Success! The Glenn Bland Method* , a book which identified the areas of spiritual, financial, educational and recreational. From this start we have added other categories and changed the names from time to time. However, when we discovered Bobb Biehl's seven categories, they matched so well with our own that we decided to keep our materials compatible with his. We highly recommend that you obtain copies of his works.

SELF-EVALUATION

1. Bobb Biehl, *Increasing Your Leadership Confidence* (Sisters, OR: Questar Publishers, 1989), 36-38. In the chapter on "Balance," Bobb offers several thoughtful questions which we have adapted for this section of the Self-Evaluation.

POSSESSIONS

1. Chuck's wife, Gwen Goldberg, is a research psychologist. After comparing more than a dozen personality inventories, Gwen concluded that the components of these different personality descriptions could all be distilled into one of four basic temperament types. Therefore, we have chosen to create a personality inventory that corresponds to this standard.
2. If you want additional information on understanding and identifying aspects of human personalities we recommend reading Ken Voges and Ron Braund's book, *Understanding How Others Misunderstand You* (Chicago, IL: Moody Press, 1990).
3. David D. Durey, *Steps Toward Spiritual Growth* (Portland, OR: Foundation of Hope, 1996), 61-74. This book provides a short study regarding the use and purpose of spiritual gifts, definitions and scripture references for each of the spiritual gifts and a spiritual gift discovery test.

MENTORING CHECKLIST

1. Adapted from the items listed for a mentor/protégé session by Bobb Biehl, Jerry "Chip" MacGregor and Glen Urquhart, in their booklet, *Mentoring, How to Find a Mentor and How to Become One* (Lake Mary, FL: Masterplanning Group International, 1994), 9.

BIBLIOGRAPHY

The following resources have either been consulted in the creation of this mentoring workbook or are suggested reading for increased personal growth and effectiveness in mentoring the Seven Areas of Life Management.

Baerg, Kevin. *Created For Execllence: 12 Keys to Godly Success*. Tacoma, WA: Inspiration Ministries, 1996.

Biehl, Bob. *Increasing Your Leadership Confidence*. Sisters, OR: Questar Publishers, 1989.
_____. Jerry "Chip" MacGregor and Glen Urquhart. *Mentoring, How to Find a Mentor and How to Become One*. Lake Mary, FL: Masterplanning Group International, 1994.
_____. Mentoring: *Confidence In Finding a Mentor and Becoming One*. Nashville: Broadman and Holman Publishers, 1996.

Bland, Glenn. *Success! The Glenn Bland Method*. Wheaton, IL: Tyndale House Publishers, 1972.

Bright, Bill. *The Secret: How to Live With Purpose and Power*. San Bernardino: Here's Life Publishers, 1989.
_____. *Witnessing Without Fear: How to Share Your Faith With Confidence*. San Bernardino: Here's Life Publishers, 1987.

Coleman, Robert E. *The Master Plan of Evangelism*. Old Tappan, NJ: Fleming H. Revell Company, 1964.

Clinton, J. Robert. *The Making of a Leader*. Colorado Springs, CO: NavPress, 1988.

Douglass, Stephen B. *How To Achieve Your Potential and Enjoy Life*. San Bernardino: Here's Life Publishers, 1987.
_____. *Managing Yourself*. San Bernardino: Here's Life Publishers, 1978.

Eims, Leroy. *The Lost Art of Disciple Making.* Grand Rapids, MI:
Zondervan Publishing House, 1978.

Elmore, Tim. *Mentoring: How to Invest Your Life in Others.*
Indianapolis, IN: Wesleyan Publishing House and Kingdom
Publishing House, 1995.
_____. *The Greatest Mentors in the Bible, 32 Relationships God
Used to Change the World.* Denver, CO: Kingdom Publishing
House, 1996.

Fee, Gordon. *How To Read the Bible For All Its Worth.* Zondervan,
1982.

Galloway, Dale. *Dare To Discipline Yourself.* Old Tappan, NJ:
Fleming H. Revell Company, 1984.

Hinckley, K.C., ed. *A Compact Guide to the Christian Life.*
Colorado Springs: NavPress, 1989.

Howard, J. Grant. *Balancing Life's Demands: A New Perspective on
Priorities.* Portland, OR: Multnomah Press, 1983.

Little, Paul E. *How to Give Away Your Faith.* Downers Grove, IL:
Inter-Varsity Press, 1966.
_____. *Know What You Believe.* Wheaton, IL: Victor Books, 1970.

Maxwell, John. *Developing The Leader Within You.* Nashville:
Thomas Nelson Publishers, 1993.
_____. *Developing The Leaders Around You.* Nashville: Thomas
Nelson Publishers, 1995.

McDonald, Gordon. *Ordering Your Private World.* 2nd ed.
Nashville: Oliver Nelson, 1985.

McDowell, Josh, ed. *Evidence That Demands a Verdict: Historical
Evidences for the Christian Faith.* San Bernardino: Here's Life
Publishers, 1979.

McPherson, Greg and Candy and Bobb and Cheryl Biehl. *Preventing Divorce*. Portland, OR: Multnomah Press, 1989.

Mears, Henrietta C.. Rev. Ed. *What the Bible Is All About*. Regal Books, 1983.

Sherman, Doug and William Hendricks. *How To Balance Competing Time Demands*. Colorado Springs, CO: NavPress, 1989.
_____ . *How To Succeed Where It Really Counts*. Colorado Springs, CO: NavPress, 1989.

Stanley, Paul D. and J. Robert Clinton. *Connecting: The Mentoring Relationships You Need to Succeed In Life*. Colorado Springs, CO: NavPress, 1992.

Stanton, Sybil. *The 25 Hour Woman*. Old Tappan, NJ: Fleming H. Revell Company, 1986.

Voges, Ken and Ron Braund. *Understanding How Others Misunderstand You*. Chicago: Moody Press, 1990.

White, Joe. *Faith Training: Raising Kids Who Love The Lord*. Colorado Springs: Focus On The Family, 1994.

RESOURCES

RESOURCES FOR SMALL GROUP MINISTRY

52 Lessons for Small Groups - Book One

52 Lessons for Small Groups - Book Two

Principles for Effective Small Group Leadership (An audio learning system for small group leaders and coaches)

Lay Pastor and Small Group Ministry Manual

RESOURCES FOR MENTORING AND EQUIPPING

Steps Toward Spiritual Growth: One-to-one Mentoring for Effective Spiritual Development

Steps Toward Ministry: One-to-one Mentoring for Effective Ministry

Steps Toward Balancing Life's Demands: One-to-one Mentoring for Effective Living

Ministry Contact Records: A Journal for Lay Pastors and Small Group Leaders

FOR ORDERS, SEMINARS OR ADDITIONAL INFORMATION:

FOUNDATION OF HOPE
11731 SE Stevens Road
Portland, OR 97266
888-248-3545
503-659-5683

Resource Order Form
Foundation of Hope
11731 SE Stevens Rd.
Portland, OR 97266

Toll free (888) 248-3545   (503) 513-0282   Fax (503) 659-3993

Quantity	Resource	Price	Total
	Mentoring Tool Books		
__Packs of 2	Steps Toward Spiritual Growth	$18/pack	$
__Packs of 2	Steps Toward Ministry	$18/pack	$
__Packs of 2	Steps Toward Balancing Life's Demands	$18/pack	$
__Packs of 6	Special Mentoring Package 2 each of the above 3 books	$50/pack	$
	Bible Study Lessons		
__Each	52 Lessons for Small Groups - Book One	$20 each	$
__Each	52 Lessons for Small Groups - Book Two	$20 each	$
Shipping and Handling Costs. Add 10% *($5.00 minimum)*			$
TOTAL AMOUNT DUE *(U.S. Funds only)*			$

Name:	Day ph# ( )	Eve ph# ( )
Church:	Church ph# ( )	
Address (Church or Home - circle one):		
City:	State:	Zip:
Method of payment (circle one): Bill Check Cash: $		MC/VISA
Charge card #: - - -	Exp. Date: /	

❏ I am interested in the October, 1998 Church Growth Conference.

❏ I am interested in having a seminar on Small Groups/Mentoring at my church.

❏ I am interested in the "Becoming Soul Mates" seminar with Drs. Les and Leslie Parrot.